Art History Review

150 trivia Questions and Answers

James Magee

Other books by this author can be found at www.littrivia.com

The aim of this book . . .

Art History Review will be the fifth book in a series of books subtitled Review-Remember-Recognize. The first book is titled American History. The second book was titled World History. The third and fourth books were respectively titled The Constitution of the United States and Classic Novels (Authors and their Titles). The sixth book will be titled Who Wrote this Book? The 150 questions and answers in this book cover paintings, the artist who painted the paintings along with their birth and death dates and the schools they represent.

This work examines a sample of the most well-known and respected paintings, sculpture and architecture of Western Civilization. Since each question is randomly chosen, the book can be opened to any page at any time.

"A great artist is always before his time or behind it."

George Edward Moore

QUESTION # 1

Who painted the most famous **The Last Supper?** Was it Leonardo da Vinci, Pablo Picasso or Paul Klee?

QUESTION # 2

Who painted **Number 5**? Was it Georges Braque, Jackson Pollock or Titian?

ANSWER # 1

The Last Supper was painted by the Italian Renaissance artist Leonardo da Vinci (1452-1519).

ANSWER # 2

Number 5 was painted by the American Abstract Expressionist artist Jackson Pollock. (1912-1956).

QUESTION # 3

Who painted **Las Meninas?** Was it Pierre-Auguste Renoir, Marc Chagall or Diego Velazquez?

QUESTION # 4

Who painted **Blueboy**? Was it Thomas Gainsborough, Michelangelo or Winslow Homer?

ANSWER # 3

Las Meninas was painted by the Spanish Baroque artist Diego Velazquez (1599-1660).

ANSWER # 4

Blueboy was painted by the English School artist Thomas Gainsborough (1727-1788).

QUESTION # 5

Who painted **Woman with the Hat?** Was it Norman Rockwell, Henri Matisse or Willem De Kooning?

QUESTION # 6

Who painted **The Lacemaker**? Was it Mary Cassatt, Marcel Duchamp or Johannes Vermeer?

ANSWER # 5

Woman with a Hat was painted by the French Fauvist artist Henri Matisse (1869-1954).

ANSWER # 6

The Lacemaker was painted by the Dutch Baroque/Dutch Golden Age artist Johannes Vermeer (1632-1675).

QUESTION # 7

Who painted **Olympia**? Was it Edouard Manet, Thomas Hart Benton or Georgia O'Keefe?

QUESTION # 8

Who painted **Leda and the Swan**? Was it Joshua Reynolds, Jacopo Tintoretto or Max Ernst?

ANSWER # 7

Olympia was painted by the French Impressionist artist Edouard Manet (1832-1888).

ANSWER # 8

Leda and the Swan was painted by the Italian High Renaissance artist Jacopo Tintoretto (1518-1594).

QUESTION # 9

Who painted **The Smoke Signal**? Was it Franz Hals, Camille Pissarro or Frederic Remington?

QUESTION # 10

Who painted **Telephone Booths**? Was it Titian, Amedeo Modigliani or Richard Estes?

ANSWER # 9

The Smoke Signal was painted by the American artist Frederic Remington (1861-1909).

ANSWER # 10

Telephone Booths was painted by the American superrealist artist Richard Estes (b. 1932).

QUESTION # 11

Who painted **Seated Man**? Was it Andy
Warhol, Peter Max, or Jackson Pollock?

QUESTION # 12

Who painted **The Hare**? Was it Frederic
Remington, Jan van Eyck or Albrecht Durer?

ANSWER # 11

Seated Man was painted by the American Pop Art artist Peter Max (b. 1937).

ANSWER # 12

The Hare was painted by the German artist Albrecht Durer (1471-1578).

QUESTION # 13

Who painted **The Starry Night**? Was it Paul Cezanne, Vincent Van Gogh, or Edouard Manet?

QUESTION # 14

Who painted **Les Demoiselles d'Avignon**? Was it Giotto di Bondone, El Greco or Pablo Picasso?

ANSWER # 13

The Starry Night was painted by the Dutch Post-Impressionist painter Vincent Van Gogh (1853-1890).

ANSWER # 14

Les Demoiselles d'Avignon was painted by the Spanish Cubist painter Pablo Picasso (1881-1973).

QUESTION # 15

Who painted **David Playing Before Saul**?
Was it Cavallino, Marc Chagall or Marcel
Duchamp?

QUESTION # 16

Who painted **Night Watch**? Was it Joshua
Reynolds, Edward Hopper or Rembrandt?

David Playing Before Saul was painted by the Italian artist Cavallino (1616-1656).

Night **Watch** was painted by the Dutch Baroque painter Rembrandt (1606-1669).

QUESTION # 17

Who painted **Mrs. Siddons**? Was it John Singer Sargent, Jasper Johns or Joshua Reynolds?

QUESTION # 18

Who painted **Peasants**? Was it painted by Diego Rivera, Thomas Gainsborough or Joshua Reynolds?

ANSWER # 17

Mrs. Siddons was painted by the English, portrait artist Joshua Reynolds (1723 1792).

ANSWER # 18

Peasants was painted by the Mexican social realism mural artist Diego Rivera (1886-1975).

QUESTION # 19

Who painted **The Card Players**? Was it Paul Cezanne, Sandro Botticelli or Franz Hals the Elder?

QUESTION # 20

Who painted **Nude Descending a Staircase**? Was it Giotto di Bondone, Giorgione or Marcel Duchamp?

ANSWER # 19

The Card Players was painted by the French Post-Impressionist artist Paul Cezanne (1839-1906).

ANSWER # 20

Nude Descending a Staircase was painted by French Dada artist Marcel Duchamp (1887-1968).

QUESTION # 21

Who painted **Madame Pompadour**? Was it
Edouard Manet, Amedeo Modigliani or
Johannes van Eyck?

QUESTION # 22

Who painted **The Persistence of Memory**?
Was it painted by Joan Miro, Salvatore Dali, or
Max Ernst?

ANSWER # 21

Madame Pompadour was painted by the Italian artist Amedeo Modigliani (1884-1920).

ANSWER # 22

The Persistence of Memory was painted by the Spanish Surrealist artist Salvatore Dali (1904-1989).

QUESTION # 23

Who painted **NightHawks**? Was it Edward Hopper, Norman Rockwell or Grant Wood?

QUESTION # 24

Who painted **Gloucester Harbor**? Was it Winslow Homer, Claude Monet or Edouard Manet?

ANSWER # 23

NightHawks was painted by the 20th Century American Realism artist Edward Hopper (1882-1967).

ANSWER # 24

Gloucester Harbor was painted by the American artist Winslow Homer (1836-1910).

QUESTION # 25

Who painted **Water Lilies**? Was it Claude
Monet, Edward Hicks or Georgia O'Keefe?

QUESTION # 26

Who painted **Two Tahitian Women**? Was it
Johannes Vermeer, Vincent Van Gogh or Paul
Gauguin?

ANSWER # 25

Water Lilies was painted by the French Impressionistic artist Claude Monet (1840-1926).

ANSWER # 26

Two Tahitian Women was painted by the French Post-Impressionist painter Paul Gauguin (1848-1903).

QUESTION # 27

Who painted **La Maja Denuda**?   Was it Francisco Goya, Titian or Fra Angelico?

QUESTION # 28

Who painted **View of Toledo**? Was it Henri Rousseau, El Greco or Edward Hopper?

ANSWER # 27

La Maja Denuda was painted by the Spanish artist Francisco Goya (1848-1903).

ANSWER # 28

View of Toledo was painted by the Cretian-born Mannerist painter El Greco (1541-1614).

QUESTION # 29

Who painted **The Theater Box**? Was it Roy Lichtenstein, Frederic Bazille or Claude Monet?

QUESTION # 30

Who painted **The Reader?** Was it Jean-Honore Fragonard, Joan Miro or Marc Chagall?

ANSWER # 29

The Theater Box was painted by the French painter Pierre-Auguste Renoir (1841-1919).

ANSWER # 30

The Reader was painted by the French artist Jean-Honore Fragonard (1732-1806).

QUESTION # 31

Who painted **Campbell's Soup Cans**? Was it Andy Warhol, Jasper Johns or Peter Max?

QUESTION # 32

Who painted **Jallais Hill, Pontoise**? Was it Giorgione, Camille Pissarro or Giotto di Bondone?

ANSWER # 31

Campbell's Soup Cans was painted by the American Pop Art artist Andy Warhol (1928-1987).

ANSWER # 32

Jallais Hill, Pontoise was painted by the French-Danish Impressionist artist Camille Pissarro (1830-1903).

QUESTION # 33

Who painted **The Boating Party?** Was it painted by Edgar Degas, Mary Cassatt or Winslow Homer?

QUESTION # 34

Who sculptured **The Thinker**? Was it Pablo Picasso, Henri de Toulouse-Lautrec or Auguste Rodin?

ANSWER # 33

The Boating Party was painted by the American-born Impressionist artist Mary Cassatt (1845-1926).

ANSWER # 34

The Thinker was sculptured by the French sculptor Auguste Rodin (1840-1917).

QUESTION # 35

Who painted the **Ville de Avray**? Was it Jean-Baptiste-Camille Corot, Hiermonymus Bosch or Gustave Courbet?

QUESTION # 36

Who painted **Noah's Ark**?   Was it painted by Marcel Duchamp, Edward Hicks or Georgia O'Keefe?

ANSWER # 35

The **Ville de Avray** was painted by the Romantic/Realist French painter Jean-Baptiste-Camille Corot (1796-1875).

ANSWER # 36

Noah's Ark was painted by the American artist Edward Hicks (1780-1849).

QUESTION # 37

Who painted **The Suburbs**? Was it Georges Seurat, Norman Rockwell or Peter Max?

QUESTION # 38

Who painted **Ballet Rehearsal**?   Was it Joshua Reynolds, Edgar Degas or Jackson Pollock?

ANSWER # 37

The Suburbs was painted by the French Pointillist painter Georges Seurat (1859-1891).

ANSWER # 38

Ballet Rehearsal was painted by the French Impressionist artist Edgar Degas (1834-1917).

QUESTION # 39

Who painted **Saint George Slaying the Dragon**? Was it Raphael, Claude Monet or Pablo Picasso?

QUESTION # 40

Who painted **Woman with a Guitar**? Was it Johannes van Eyck, Georges Braque or Anthony van Dyck?

ANSWER # 39

Saint George Slaying the Dragon was painted by the Italian High Renaissance painter Raphael (1483-1520).

ANSWER # 40

Woman with a Guitar was painted by the French Fauvist artist Georges Braque (1882-1963).

QUESTION # 41

Who painted the **Moulin Rouge: La Goulue**?
Was it Edouard Manet, Henri de Toulouse-
Lautrec or Diego Rivera?

QUESTION # 42

Who sculptured **St. John Baptiste
Preaching**?   Was it sculptured by Pablo
Picasso, Rodin or Georges Braque?

ANSWER # 41

Moulin Rouge: La Goulue was painted by the French Post-Impressionist painter Henri de Toulouse-Lautrec (1864-1901).

ANSWER # 42

St. John Baptiste Preaching was sculptured by the French sculptor Auguste Rodin (1840-1917).

QUESTION # 43

Who sculptured the **Pieta**? Was it Michelangelo, Pablo Picasso or Auguste Rodin?

QUESTION # 44

Who painted **The Lawrence Tree**? Was it Georgia O'Keefe, Thomas Hart Benton or Grandma Moses?

ANSWER # 43

The **Pieta** was sculptured by the Italian Renaissance artist Michelangelo (1452-1519).

ANSWER # 44

The Lawrence Tree was painted by the American modernist artist Georgia O'Keefe (1887-1986).

QUESTION # 45

Who painted **Portrait of a Man in a Red Cap**? Was it painted by Henri Matisse, Titian or Paul Gauguin?

QUESTION # 46

Who painted **The Sunblind**? Was it Jackson Pollock, Juan Gris or Andy Warhol?

ANSWER # 45

Portrait of a Man in a Red Cap was painted by the Italian High Renaissance artist Titian (1488-1576).

ANSWER # 46

The Sunblind was painted by the Spanish Cubism artist Juan Gris (1887-1927).

QUESTION # 47

Who designed the **Solomon R. Guggenheim Museum**? Was it Ludwig Mies van der Rohe, I. M. Pei or Frank Lloyd Wright?

QUESTION # 48

Who painted **Beautiful World**? Was it painted by Vincent van Gogh, Grandma Moses or Paul Gauguin?

ANSWER # 47

The **Solomon R. Guggenheim Museum** was designed by the American architect Frank Lloyd Wright (1867-1959).

ANSWER # 48

Beautiful World was painted by the American artist Grandma Moses [Anna Mary Moses] (1860-1961).

QUESTION # 49

Who painted **Embarkation**? Was it Thomas Hart Benton, Grant Wood or Andrew Wyeth?

QUESTION # 50

Who sculptured **David**? Was it Pablo Picasso, Auguste Rodin or Michelangelo?

ANSWER # 49

Embarkation was painted by the American Realist artist Thomas Hart Benton (1889-1975).

ANSWER # 50

David was sculptured by the Italian Renaissance sculptor Michelangelo (1475-1564).

QUESTION # 51

Who painted **A Girl with a Water Can**?   Was it painted by Andy Warhol, Pierre-Auguste Renoir or William Hogarth?

QUESTION # 52

Who painted **The Twittering Machine**? Was it Paul Klee, Norman Rockwell or Edward Hopper?

ANSWER # 51

A Girl with a Water Can was painted by the French Impressionist artist Pierre-Auguste Renoir (1841-1919).

ANSWER # 52

The Twittering Machine was painted by the French, Expressionist/Surrealist artist Paul Klee (1879-1940).

QUESTION # 53

Who designed **The National Gallery East Building**? Was it I. M. Pei, Frank Lloyd Wright or Ludwig Mies van der Rohe?

QUESTION # 54

Who painted **The Milkmaid**?   Was it painted by Johannes Vermeer, Marcel Duchamp or Piet Mondrian?

ANSWER # 53

The National Gallery East Building was designed by Chinese American architect I. M. Pei (b. 1917).

ANSWER # 54

The Milkmaid was painted by the Dutch Baroque/Dutch Golden Age artist Johannes Vermeer (1632-1675).

QUESTION # 55

Who painted **American Gothic**? Was it Grant Wood, Georgia O'Keefe or Thomas Hart Benton?

QUESTION # 56

Who painted **Broadway Boogie Woogie?** Was it Piet Mondrian, Pablo Picasso or Juan Gris?

ANSWER # 55

American Gothic was painted by the American Realist artist Grant Wood (1892-1942).

ANSWER # 56

Broadway Boogie Woogie was painted by the Dutch artist of the De Stijl school, Piet Mondrian (1872-1944).

QUESTION # 57

Who painted **Knight, Death, and the Devil**? Was it painted by Tintoretto, Titian or Albrecht Durer?

QUESTION # 58

Who painted **The Helga Pictures**? Was it James Abbott McNeil Whistler, Andrew Wyeth or John Singer Sargent?

ANSWER # 57

Knight, Death, and the Devil was painted by the German artist Albrecht Durer (1471-1578).

ANSWER # 58

The Helga Pictures was painted by the American Realist artist Andrew Wyeth (1917-2009).

QUESTION # 59

Who painted **Willie Gillis**? Was it painted by Jasper Johns, Norman Rockwell or Grant Wood?

QUESTION # 60

Who painted **The Bridle Path**?   Was it painted by Edouard Manet, Winslow Homer or Frederic Remington?

ANSWER # 59

Willie Gillis was painted by the American Realist artist Norman Rockwell (1894-1978).

ANSWER # 60

The Bridle Path was painted by the American artist Winslow Homer (1836-1910).

QUESTION # 61

Who designed the **Barcelona Pavilion**? Was it I. M. Pei, Frank Lloyd Wright or Ludwig Mies van der Rohe?

QUESTION # 62

Who painted **A Burial at Ornans**? Was it Gustave Courbet, Andrew Wyeth or William Hogarth?

ANSWER # 61

The **Barcelona Pavilion** was designed by the German architect Ludwig Mies van der Rohe (1886-1969).

ANSWER # 62

A Burial at Ornans was painted by the French Realist Gustave Courbet (1819-1877).

QUESTION # 63

Who painted **The Astronomer**?   Was it painted by Johannes Vermeer, Piet Mondrian or Norman Rockwell?

QUESTION # 64

Who painted **Flag**? Was it painted by Jackson Pollock, Max Ernst or Jasper Johns?

ANSWER # 63

The Astronomer was painted by the Dutch Baroque/Dutch Golden Age artist Johannes Vermeer (1632-1675).

ANSWER # 64

Flag was painted by the American Abstract Expressionist artist Jasper Johns (b. 1930).

QUESTION # 65

Who painted **Woman III**? Was it Wilhelm de Kooning, Marc Chagall or Pablo Picasso?

QUESTION # 66

Who painted **The Papal Palace, Avignon**? Was it painted by Titian, Paul Signac or Fra Angelico?

ANSWER # 65

Women III was painted by the Dutch American Abstract Expressionistic artist Wilhelm de Kooning (1904-1977).

ANSWER # 66

The Papal Palace, Avignon was painted by the French Neo-Impressionist artist who worked with Georges Seurat on Pointillism (1859-1891).

QUESTION # 67

Who painted **I and the Village?** Was it Marc Chagall, Pablo Picasso or Andre Derain?

QUESTION # 68

Who painted **Lane Near a Small Town**? Was it Alfred Sisley, Edgar Degas or Camille Pissarro?

ANSWER # 67

I and the Village was painted by the French-Jewish Belarusian modern figurative artist Marc Chagall (1887-1985).

ANSWER # 68

Lane Near a Small Town was painted by the French Impressionist artist Alfred Sisley (1839-1899).

QUESTION # 69

Who painted **The Blue Rider**?   Was it painted by Georgia O'Keefe, Andy Warhol or Wassily Kandinsky?

QUESTION # 70

Who painted **Arrangement in Grey and Black: Portrait of the Artist's Mother**? Was it John Singer Sargent, Joshua Reynolds or James Abbott McNeil Whistler?

ANSWER # 69

The Blue Rider was painted by the Russian Abstract Expressionist artist Wassily Kandinsky (1866-1944).

ANSWER # 70

Arrangement in Grey and Black: Portrait of the Artist's Mother was painted by the American Tonalist James Abbott McNeil Whistler (1834-1903).

QUESTION # 71

Who painted **The Gleaners**? Was it Honore Daumier, Jean Francois Millet or Jean-Baptiste-Camille Corot?

QUESTION # 72

Who painted **The Peasant Wedding**?   Was it painted by Diego Velazquez, Pieter Bruegel or Diego Rivera?

ANSWER # 71

The Gleaners was painted by the French Realist artist Jean Francois Millet (1814-1875).

ANSWER # 72

The Peasant Wedding was painted by the Belgian artist Pieter Bruegel the Elder during the Dutch Flemish Renaissance (c. 1525-1569).

QUESTION # 73

Who painted **Christ Entry into Brussels**? Was it James Ensor, Ferdinand Hodler or Odilon Redon?

QUESTION # 74

Who painted **Paris: A Rainy Day**? Was it Gustave Caillebotte, Camille Pissarro or Jean-Baptiste-Camille Corot?

ANSWER # 73

Christ's Entry into Brussels was painted by the Flemish-Belgian artist James Ensor (c. 1860-1949).

ANSWER # 74

Paris: A Rainy Day was painted by the French Impressionist artist Gustave Caillebotte (1848-1894)

QUESTION # 75

Who painted **The Exchange of Princesses**?
Was it painted by El Greco, Peter Paul
Reubens of Wilhelm de Kooning?

QUESTION # 76

Who painted the **Mona Lisa?** Was it
Leonardo da Vinci, Pablo Picasso or
Michelangelo?

ANSWER # 75

The Exchange of Princesses was painted by the Flemish Baroque artist Peter Paul Reubens (1577-1640).

ANSWER # 76

The **Mona Lisa** was painted by the Italian Renaissance artist Leonardo da Vinci (1452-1519).

QUESTION # 77

Who painted **The Deep**?   Was it Frederic Remington, Jackson Pollock or Thomas Hart Benton?

QUESTION # 78

Who painted **The Lamentation of Christ**? Was it painted by Pierre-Auguste Renoir, Marc Chagall or Giotto di Bondone?

ANSWER # 77

The Deep was painted by the American Abstract Expressionist artist Jackson Pollock (1912-1956).

ANSWER # 78

The Lamentation of Christ was painted by the late Gothic Italian artist Giotto di Bondone (c. 1266-1337).

QUESTION # 79

Who painted **Mr. and Mrs. Andrews**? Was it Thomas Gainsborough, Michelangelo or Winslow Homer?

QUESTION # 80

Who painted **The Snail**? Was it Norman Rockwell, Henri Matisse or Willem De Kooning?

ANSWER # 79

Mr. and Mrs. Andrews was painted by the English School artist Thomas Gainsborough (1727-1788).

ANSWER # 80

The Snail was painted by the French Fauvist artist Henri Matisse (1869-1954).

QUESTION # 81

Who painted **The Arnofini Portrait**?   Was it painted by Thomas Hart Benton, Georgia O'Keefe or Jan van Eyck?

QUESTION # 82

Who painted **The Luncheon on the Grass**? Was it Edward Hicks, Vincent Van Gogh or Edouard Manet?

ANSWER # 81

The Arnofini Portrait was painted by the Flemish Renaissance artist Jan van Eyck (c. 1395-1441).

ANSWER # 82

The Luncheon on the Grass was painted by the French Impressionist artist Edouard Manet (1832-1888).

QUESTION # 83

Who painted **The Siege of Asola**? Was it Joshua Reynolds, Jacopo Tintoretto or Max Ernst?

QUESTION # 84

Who painted **The Virgin of the Annunciation**?   Was it Franz Hals, Camille Pissarro or Fra Angelico?

The Siege of Asola was painted by the Italian High Renaissance artist Jacopo Tintoretto (1518-1594).

ANSWER # 84

The Virgin of the Annunciation was painted by the early Renaissance Italian artist Fra Angelico (c. 1395-1455).

QUESTION # 85

Who painted **Coming from the Mill**? Was it L. S. Lowry, Winslow Homer or Norman Rockwell?

QUESTION # 86

Who painted **Portrait of a German Officer**? Was it Frederic Remington, Edward Hicks or Marsden Hartley?

ANSWER # 85

Coming from the Mill was painted by the Northern England urban landscape artist L. S. [Laurence Stephen] Lowry (1887-1976).

ANSWER # 86

Portrait of a German Officer was painted by the American modernist artist Marsden Hartley (1877- 1943).

QUESTION # 87

Who painted **The Birth of Venus**? Was it painted by Vincent Van Gogh, Edouard Manet or Sandro Botticelli?

QUESTION # 88

Who painted **Café Terrace at Night**? Was it Paul Cezanne, Vincent Van Gogh, or Eduoard Monet?

ANSWER # 87

The Birth of Venus was painted by the Italian Renaissance artist Sandro Botticelli (c. 1445-1510).

ANSWER # 88

Café Terrace at Night was painted by the Dutch Post-Impressionist painter Vincent Van Gogh (1853-1890).

QUESTION # 89

Who painted **Guernica**? Was it Giotto di
Bondone, El Greco or Pablo Picasso?

QUESTION # 90

Who painted **Sleeping Venus**? Was it
painted by Georgia O'Keefe, Andrew Wyeth or
Giorgione?

ANSWER # 89

Guernica was painted by the Spanish Cubist painter Pablo Picasso (1881-1973).

ANSWER # 90

Sleeping Venus was painted by the Italian High Renaissance artist Giorgione (c. 1477-1510).

QUESTION # 91

Who painted **Sydics of the Cloth Merchant's Guild**? Was it Joshua Reynolds, Edward Hopper or Rembrandt?

QUESTION # 92

Who painted **The Age of Innocence**? Was it John Singer Sargent, Jasper Johns or Joshua Reynolds?

Sydics of the Cloth Merchant's Guild was painted by the Dutch Baroque painter Rembrandt (1606-1669).

ANSWER # 92

The Age of Innocence was painted by the English, portrait artist Joshua Reynolds (1723 1792).

QUESTION # 93

Who painted **Portrait of Erasmus of Rotterdam**?   Was it painted by Claude Monet, Pablo Picasso or Hans Holbein the Younger?

QUESTION # 94

Who painted **Apples and Oranges**? Was it painted by Paul Cezanne, Juan Gris or Georges Braque?

ANSWER # 93

Portrait of Erasmus of Rotterdam was painted by the Northern Renaissance German artist Hans Holbein the Younger (c. 1498-1543).

ANSWER # 94

Apples and Oranges was painted by the French Post-Impressionist artist Paul Cezanne (1839-1906).

QUESTION # 95

Who painted **Fountain**? Was it painted by Juan Gris, Fernand Leger or Marcel Duchamp?

QUESTION # 96

Who painted **The Garden of Earthly Delights**?   Was it painted by Hieronymus Bosch, Vincent van Gogh or Paul Gauguin?

ANSWER # 95

Fountain was painted by the French Dada artist Marcel Duchamp (1887-1968).

ANSWER # 96

The Garden of Earthly Delights was painted by the Early Netherlandish Renaissance artist Hieronymus Bosch [Jeroen Arthoniszoon van Aiken] (1450-1560).

QUESTION # 97

Who painted the **Crucifixion**? Was it painted by Joan Miro, Salvatore Dali, or Jackson Pollock?

QUESTION # 98

Who painted **Automat**? Was it Edward Hopper, Norman Rockwell or Grant Wood?

ANSWER # 97

The **Crucifixion** was painted by the Spanish Surrealist artist Salvatore Dali (1904-1989).

ANSWER # 98

Automat was painted by the 20th Century Realism artist Edward Hopper (1882-1967).

QUESTION # 99

Who painted **Children's Games**?   Was it painted by Claude Monet, Edouard Manet or Pieter Bruegel?

QUESTION # 100

Who painted **Morning Haze**? Was it painted by Claude Monet, Anthony van Dyck or Vincent Van Gogh?

ANSWER # 99

Children's Games was painted by the Belgian artist Pieter Bruegel the Elder during the Dutch Flemish Renaissance (1525-1569).

ANSWER # 100

Morning Haze was painted by the French Impressionist artist Claude Monet (1840-1926).

QUESTION # 101

Who painted **Still Life with Three Puppies**?
Was it John Jaspers, Edward Hopper or Paul
Gauguin?

QUESTION # 102

Who painted **Saint Francis of Assisi in
Ecstasy**? Was it painted by Caravaggio,
Alfred Sisley or Edward Hopper?

ANSWER # 101

Still Life with Three Puppies was painted by the French Post-Impressionist painter Paul Gauguin (1848-1903).

ANSWER # 102

Saint Francis of Assisi in Ecstasy was painted by the Italian Baroque artist Caravaggio (1571-1610).

QUESTION # 103

Who painted **The Dream of Philip II**? Was it Johannes Vermeer, El Greco or Hans Holbein the Younger?

QUESTION # 104

Who painted **Bathers**? Was it Frederic Bazille, Pierre-Auguste Renoir or Winslow Homer?

ANSWER # 103

The Dream of Philip II was painted by the Cretian-born Mannerist painter El Greco (1541-1614).

ANSWER # 104

Bathers was painted by the French Impression painter Pierre-Auguste Renoir (1841-1919).

QUESTION # 105

Who painted **The Elevation of the Cross**? Was it painted by Salvatore Dali, Peter Paul Reubens or Marc Chagall?

QUESTION # 106

Who painted **Money**? Was it painted by Andy Warhol, Jasper Johns or Peter Max?

ANSWER # 105

The Elevation of the Cross was painted by the Flemish Baroque artist Peter Paul Reubens (1577-1640).

ANSWER # 106

Money was painted by the American Pop Art artist Andy Warhol (1928-1987).

QUESTION # 107

Who painted **Two Women Chatting by the Sea**? Was it Georges Braque, Camille Pissarro or Juan Gris?

QUESTION # 108

Who painted **Samson and Delilah?**   Was it Claude Monet, Pablo Picasso or Van Dyck?

Two Women Chatting by the Sea was painted by the French-Danish Impressionist artist Camille Pissarro (1803-1903).

ANSWER # 108

Samson and Delilah was painted by the Flemish Baroque artist Anthony van Dyck (1599-1641).

QUESTION # 109

Who sculptured **The Age of Bronze**? Was it Pablo Picasso, Edgar Degas or Auguste Rodin?

QUESTION # 110

Who painted the **A Cow and its Keepers**? Was it Jean-Baptiste-Camille Corot, Camille Pissarro or Gustave Courbet?

ANSWER # 109

The Age of Bronze was sculptured by the French sculptor Auguste Rodin (1840-1917).

ANSWER # 110

A Cow and its Keepers was painted by the Romantic/Realist French painter Jean-Baptiste-Camille Corot (1796-1875).

QUESTION # 111

Who painted **Gypsy Girl**?   Was it painted by Franz Hals the Elder, Claude Monet or Pablo Picasso?

QUESTION # 112

Who painted **Sunday Afternoon on the Island of La Grande Jette**? Was it Georges Seurat, Paul Signac or Edward Hicks?

ANSWER # 111

Gypsy Girl was painted by the Golden Age Flemish Dutch artist Franz Hals the Elder (1580-1666).

ANSWER # 112

Sunday Afternoon on the Island of La Grande Jette was painted by the French Pointillist painter Georges Seurat (1859-1891).

QUESTION # 113

Who painted **Dance Class**? Was it Edgar Degas, Gramt Wood or Claude Monet?

QUESTION # 114

Who painted **Lucas**? Was it painted by Jasper Johns, Chuck [Charles] Close or Max Ernst?

ANSWER # 113

Dance Class was painted by the French Impressionist painter Edgar Degas (1834-1917).

ANSWER # 114

Lucas was painted by American Mural/Portrait artist Chuck [Charles] Close (b. 1940).

QUESTION # 115

Who painted **Fruitdish and Glass**? Was it Juan Gris, Georges Braque or Camille Pissaro?

QUESTION # 116

Who painted **Portrait of Gabrielle**? Was it Georgia O'Keefe, Andrew Wyeth or Henri de Toulouse-Lautrec?

ANSWER # 115

Fruitdish and Glass was painted by the French Fauvist artist Georges Braque (1882-1983).

ANSWER # 116

Portrait of Gabrielle was painted by the French Post-Impressionist painter Henri de Toulouse-Lautrec (1884-1901).

QUESTION # 117

Who painted **The Rocky Mountains Leader's Peak**? Was it painted by Albert Bienstadt, Paul Signac or Edouard Manet?

QUESTION # 118

Who designed the **Imperial Hotel, Tokyo**? Was it I. M. Pei, Ludwig Mies van der Rohe or Frank Lloyd Wright?

The Rocky Mountains Leader's Peak was painted by the German-American Luminist artist Albert Bienstadt (1830-1902).

The **Imperial Hotel, Tokyo** was designed by the American architect Frank Lloyd Wright (1867-1959).

QUESTION # 119

Who painted **Ram's Head, White Holyhock and Little Hills**? Was it Georgia O'Keefe, Thomas Hart Benton or Grant Wood?

QUESTION # 120

Who painted **Pilgrims Going to Church**? Was it painted by Claude Monet, Pablo Picasso or George Henry Boughton?

ANSWER # 119

Ram's Head, White Holyhock and Little Hills was painted by the American modernist artist Georgia O'Keefe (1887-1986).

ANSWER # 120

Pilgrims Going to Church was painted by the English-American artist George Henry Boughton (1833-1905).

QUESTION # 121

Who painted **Bananas**? Was it Juan Gris,
Georges Braque or Camille Pissaro?

QUESTION # 122

Who designed **The Illinois, Chicago, U.S. A.**?
Was it I. M. Pei, Frank Lloyd Wright or Ludwig
Mies van der Rohe?

Bananas was painted by the Spanish Cubism
artist Juan Gris (1887-1927).

ANSWER # 122

The Illinois, Chicago, U.S. A. was designed
by the American architect Frank Lloyd Wright
(1867-1959).

QUESTION # 123

Who painted **Tornado over Kansas**? Was it Thomas Hart Benton, John Steurt Curry or Andrew Wyeth?

QUESTION # 124

Who painted **The Ballad of the Jealous Lover of Lone Green Valley**? Was it painted by Claude Monet, Pablo Picasso or Thomas Hart Benton?

ANSWER #123

Tornado over Kansas was painted by the American Realist artist John Steuart Curry (1897-1946).

ANSWER # 124

The Ballad of the Jealous Lover of Lone Green Valley was painted by the Regionalist artist Thomas Hart Benton (1889-1975).

QUESTION # 125

Who designed **Price Tower, Oklahoma, U.S.A.**? Was it I. M. Pei, Frank Lloyd Wright or Ludwig Mies van der Rohe?

QUESTION # 126

Who painted **Marriage Feast at Cana**? Was it painted by Hiermonymus Bosch, Johannes Vermeer or Juan de Flandes?

ANSWER # 125

Price Tower, Oklahoma, U.S.A. was designed by the American architect Frank Lloyd Wright (1867-1959).

ANSWER # 126

Marriage Feast at Cana was painted by the Early Netherlands artist Juan de Flandes (c. 1460-1519).

QUESTION # 127

Who painted **Fish Magic**? Was it Marc Chagall, Edouard Manet or Paul Klee?

QUESTION # 128

Who designed The **Louvre Pyramid, Paris**? Was it I. M. Pei, Frank Lloyd Wright or Ludwig Mies van der Rohe?

Fish Magic was painted by the French Expressionist/Surrealist artist Paul Klee (1879-1940).

The **Louvre Pyramid, Paris** was designed by Chinese American architect I. M. Pei (b. 1917).

QUESTION # 129

Who painted **The Swing**?   Was it painted by Winslow Homer, Jean Honore Fragonard of William Hogarth?

QUESTION # 130

Who painted **Young Corn**? Was it Grant Wood, Georgia O'Keefe or Thomas Hart Benton?

The Swing was painted by French Rococo artist Jean Honore Fragonard (1732-1806).

Young Corn was painted by the American Realist artist Grant Wood (1892-1942).

QUESTION # 131

Who painted **Composition with Yellow, Blue and Red**? Was it Piet Mondrian, Pablo Picasso or Juan Gris?

QUESTION # 132

Who painted **M. Loulou**?   Was it painted by Francisco Goya, James Ensor or Grandma Moses?

ANSWER # 131

Composition with Yellow, Blue and Red
was painted by the Dutch artist of the De Stijl
school, Piet Mondrian (1872-1944).

ANSWER # 132

M. Loulou was painted by the Spanish artist
Francisco Goya (1848-1903).

QUESTION # 133

Who painted **The Giant**? Was it James Abbott McNeil Whistler, N. C. Wyeth or John Singer Sargent?

QUESTION # 134

Who painted **The Golden Rule**? Was it Jasper Johns, Norman Rockwell or Grant Wood?

ANSWER # 133

The Giant was painted by the American Realist artist N. C. [Newell Convers – Andrew Wyeth's father] Wyeth (1882-1945).

ANSWER # 134

The Golden Rule was painted by the American Realist artist Norman Rockwell (1894-1978).

QUESTION # 135

Who painted **Sailing the Catboat**?   Was it painted by Winslow Homer, Paul Cezanne or Paul Gauguin?

QUESTION # 136

Who designed the **IBM Plaza, Chicago, U.S.A.**? Was it I. M. Pei, Frank Lloyd Wright or Ludwig Mies van der Rohe?

ANSWER # 135

Sailing the Catboat was painted by the
American artist Winslow Homer (1836-1910).

ANSWER # 136

The **IBM Plaza, Chicago, U.S.A.** was
designed by the German architect Ludwig
Mies van der Rohe (1886-1969).

QUESTION # 137

Who painted **The Hammock**? Was it Gustave Courbet, Andrew Wyeth or Jean Francois Millet?

QUESTION # 138

Who painted **The Old Checkered House**? Was it painted by Grandma Moses, Claude Monet or Pablo Picasso?

ANSWER # 137

The Hammock was painted by the French Realist Gustave Courbet (1819-1877).

ANSWER # 138

The Old Checkered House was painted by artist Grandma Moses [Anna Mary Moses] (1860-1961).

QUESTION # 139

Who painted **Map**? Was it Jackson Pollock, Max Ernst or Jasper Johns?

QUESTION # 140

Who painted **Attic**? Was it Wilhelm de Kooning, Marc Chagall or Pablo Picasso?

ANSWER # 139

Map was painted by the American Abstract Expressionist artist Jasper Johns (b. 1930).

ANSWER # 140

Attic was painted by the Dutch American Abstract Expressionistic artist Wilhelm de Kooning (1904-1977).

QUESTION # 141

Who painted **Edward VI as a Child**?   Was it painted by Hans Holbein the Younger, Frederic Remington or Edward Hopper?

QUESTION # 142

Who painted **The Violinist**? Was it Marc Chagall, Pablo Picasso or Jackson Pollock?

?

ANSWER # 141

Edward VI as a Child was painted by German Northern Renaissance artist Hans Holbein the Younger (c. 1498-1543).

ANSWER # 142

The Violinist was painted by the French-Jewish Belarusian modern figurative artist Marc Chagall (1887-1987).

QUESTION # 143

Who painted **The Lesson**? Was it Alfred Sisley, Edgar Degas or Camille Pissarro?

QUESTION # 144

Who painted **Washington Crossing the Delaware**? Was it painted by Emanuel Gottlieb Leutze, Thomas Gainsborough or Anthony van Dyck?

ANSWER # 143

The Lesson was painted by the French Impressionist artist Alfred Sisley (1839-1899).

ANSWER # 144

Washington Crossing the Delaware was painted by German-born artist Emanuel Gottlieb Leutze (1816-1868).

QUESTION # 145

Who painted **Nocturne in Black and Gold: The Falling Rocket**? Was it John Singer Sargent, Joshua Reynolds or James Abbott McNeil Whistler?

QUESTION # 146

Who painted **The Sower**? Was it Honore Daumier, Jean Francois Millet or Jean-Baptiste-Camille Corot?

ANSWER # 145

Nocturne in Black and Gold: The Falling Rocket was painted by the American Tonalist James Abbott McNeil Whistler (1834-1903).

ANSWER # 146

The Sower was painted by the French Realist artist Jean Francois Millet (1814-1875).

QUESTION # 147

Who sculptured **Monument With Standing Beast**?   Was it sculptured by Pablo Picasso, Jean Debuffet or Auguste Rodin?

QUESTION # 148

Who painted **The Rower**? Was it James Ensor, Ferdinand Hodler or Odilon Redon?

ANSWER # 147

Monument With Standing Beast was sculptured by French sculpturer Jean Debuffet (1901-1985).

ANSWER # 148

The Rower was painted by the Flemish-Belgian artist James Ensor (c. 1860-1949).

QUESTION # 149

Who painted **Paris Street**? Was it painted by Jan van Eyck, Gustave Caillebotte or Hiermonymus Bosch?

QUESTION # 150

Who painted **The Gulf Stream**?   Was it painted by N. C. Wyeth, Joshua Reynolds or Winslow Homer?

ANSWER # 149

Paris Street was painted by the French Impressionist artist Gustave Caillebotte (1848-1894).

ANSWER # 150

The Gulf Stream was painted by the American artist Winslow Homer (1836-1810).

Books by James Magee

American History

World History

The Fifty States

World Capitals

The Constitution of the United States – America's Owner's Manual

Understanding Legal Terms/Cortroom Humor

The History of the Novel: Six Literary Periods

Classic Novels (Authors and Their Titles)

Novel Characters of Literature

Fictional Characters of Literature

Who Wrote This Book?

The Opening and Closing Lines of Novels

Classical Novels (Start . . . Finish)

Misspell or Misspell?

Shakespeare Unplugged

The Triple Crown Affair: Horseracing Basics

Basic Accounting and Finance Quiz

Psychology 101 – Part I

Psychology 101 – Part II

Philosophy 101

A Simple Guide to Philosophy

Music History Review

Rock 'n Roll Review

Motown/Female Groups/British Invasion